3. Look at the examples. Can you see what
   links the words?

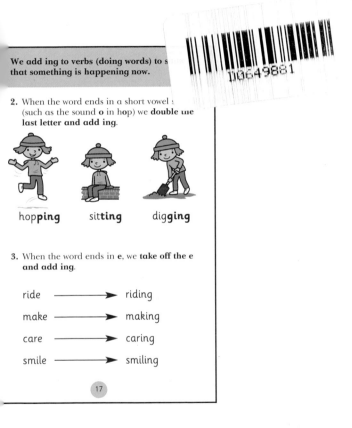

We add ing to verbs (doing words) to s...
that something is happening now.

2. When the word ends in a short vowel ...
(such as the sound **o** in hop) we **double** the
last letter and add ing.

hop**ping**   sit**ting**   dig**ging**

3. When the word ends in **e**, we **take off the e
and add ing**.

ride   ⟶   riding

make   ⟶   making

care   ⟶   caring

smile   ⟶   smiling

4. Try making up new examples of your own.

Written by Emily Guille-Marrett
Illustrated by Ian Cunliffe

Published by Ladybird Books Ltd
A Penguin Company
Penguin Books Ltd, 80 Strand, London WC2R 0RL, UK
Penguin Books Australia Ltd, Camberwell, Victoria, Australia
Penguin Books (NZ) Ltd, Cnr Airbourne and Rosedale Roads, Albany, Auckland, 1310, New Zealand

3 5 7 9 10 8 6 4 2

© LADYBIRD BOOKS MMIV

Printed in Italy

Spelling
for
School

Ladybird

Vowels and consonants

There are 26 letters in the alphabet.

Aa

Bb

Cc

Dd

Ee

Ff

Gg

Hh

Ii

Jj

Kk

Ll

Mm

Nn

Oo

Pp

Qq

Rr

Ss

Tt

Uu

Vv

Ww

Xx

Yy

Zz

Five letters in the alphabet are **vowels**.

a   e   i   o   u

The other 21 letters are **consonants**.

Every single word has at least one vowel sound in it.

These words have **short vowel sounds**.

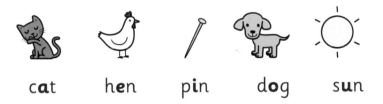

cat   hen   pin   dog   sun

These words have **long vowel sounds**.

cake   bee   kite   note   flute

Sometimes the letter **y** is used as a vowel in words such as **hymn** and **why**.

Plurals – adding s and es

We usually make nouns, or naming words, plural by adding the letter **s** to the end of the word to show more than one thing.

rabbit**s**

pen**s**

gir**ls**

book**s**

toy**s**

apple**s**

When a noun ends in the letters **s**, **x**, **sh** or **ch** we usually make it plural by adding the letters **es** to the end of the word.

bus**es**

dress**es**

fox**es**

box**es**

dish**es**

sandwich**es**

Plurals – adding ies and irregular plurals

When a noun ends in a consonant followed by the letter **y**, such as baby, we **take off the y and add** the letters **ies** to the end of the word.

bab**ies**

lorr**ies**

pupp**ies**

cherr**ies**

fair**ies**

jell**ies**

We use plurals to show more than one thing.

Some words do not follow a rule when they are made plural. You just have to learn these words.

Singular (one thing)   **Plural** (two or more)

child   children

foot   feet

goose   geese

man   men

mouse   mice

sheep   sheep

tooth   teeth

Making an adjective by adding y

1. Adjectives are describing words such as **big** and **green**. However, we can **add y** to some nouns to make adjectives.

rainy

dirty

windy

smelly

curly

hairy

Some nouns (naming words) become adjectives (describing words) by adding the letter y.

2. When the word contains a short vowel sound (such as the sound **u** in s**u**n) we **double the last letter and add y**.

sun**ny**   mud**dy**   spot**ty**

3. When the word ends in **e**, we **take off the e and add y**.

wave	⟶	wavy
laze	⟶	lazy
stone	⟶	stony
slime	⟶	slimy

Making comparisons by adding er and est

1. We just **add er** or **est** to the end of many adjectives to compare them.

 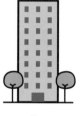 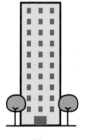

tall   tall**er**   tall**est**

 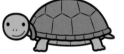

slow   slow**er**   slow**est**

soft   soft**er**   soft**est**

We add er and est to compare adjectives (describing words) with one another.

2. If the adjective ends in the letter **y**, **change the y to an i** before adding **er** or **est** to the end of the word.

dirty   dirt**ier**   dirt**iest**

funny   funn**ier**   funn**iest**

hairy   hair**ier**   hair**iest**

Changing verbs by adding ing

1. We just **add ing** to the end of many verbs to show that something is happening now.

playing

jumping

kicking

dusting

walking

looking

We add ing to verbs (doing words) to show that something is happening now.

2. When the word ends in a short vowel sound (such as the sound **o** in h**o**p) we **double the last letter and add ing.**

hop**ping**   sit**ting**   dig**ging**

3. When the word ends in **e**, we **take off the e and add ing.**

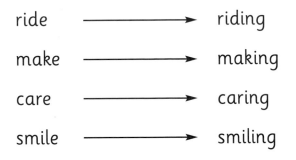

ride	riding
make	making
care	caring
smile	smiling

Changing verbs by adding ed

1. We just **add ed** to the end of many verbs to show that something has happened.

lick**ed**   talk**ed**   help**ed**

2. When the word ends in a short vowel sound (such as the sound **u** in r**u**b) we **double the last letter and add ed**.

rub**bed**   jog**ged**   clap**ped**

We add ed to verbs (doing words) to show that something has happened.

3. When the word ends in **e**, we **take off the e and add ed**.

like   ⟶   liked

hope   ⟶   hoped

care   ⟶   cared

smile   ⟶   smiled

4. Remember, some words **do not add ed** to show that something has happened in the past. Here are some examples:

can / could   give / gave   see / saw

do / did   have / had   sit / sat

eat / ate   make / made   wear / wore

get / got   run / ran   write / wrote

Adding un and other word beginnings

To make some words negative or opposite just add **un** to the beginning of a word. There are no other changes to be made to the main word.

unhappy

untie

untidy

unzip

unwell

unpack

We add certain sets of letters to the beginning of a word to change its meaning.

There are other sets of letters which can be added to the beginning of a word to change its meaning. For example:

dislike

misbehave

defrost

recycle

invisible

prehistoric

Changing the meaning by adding ful, ly and less

1. We just **add ful** to the end of many words.

colour**ful**

wonder**ful**

wish**ful**

2. We just **add ly** to the end of many words.

slow**ly**

clever**ly**

quiet**ly**

3. We just **add less** to the end of many words.

care**less**

home**less**

harm**less**

We add certain sets of letters to the end of a word to change its meaning.

If the word ends in y, **change the y to i**, and **add ful**.

plenty ⟶ plent**iful**

beauty ⟶ beaut**iful**

mercy ⟶ merc**iful**

If the word ends in y, **change the y to i**, and **add ly**.

happy ⟶ happ**ily**

angry ⟶ angr**ily**

pretty ⟶ prett**ily**

If the word ends in y, **change the y to i**, and **add less**.

penny ⟶ penn**iless**

pity ⟶ pit**iless**

mercy ⟶ merc**iless**

Homophones

A homophone is a word that sounds the same as another word but has a different spelling and meaning.

hare

hair

pair

pear

flower

flour

Words that sound the same but are spelt differently and have different meanings.

If you are unsure of the correct spelling of a homophone, use a dictionary to help you.

blew

blue

see

sea

Here are some more examples of **homophones**.

be / bee   eye / I   for / four

hear / here   to / too / two   week / weak

Homonyms

A homonym is a word that sounds the same and is spelt the same as another word but has a different meaning.

bark

bark

ring

ring

bat

bat

Words that sound the same and are spelt the same but they have different meanings.

wave   wave

jam   jam

Here are some more examples of **homonyms**.

bank   club   flat   match

park   pop   sink   watch

Compound words

A **compound word** is one long word made up of two smaller words.

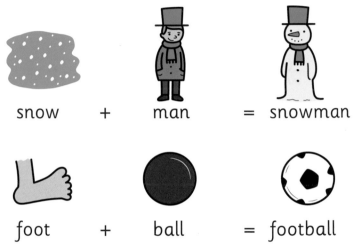

snow + man = snowman

foot + ball = football

Here are some more examples of **compound words**.

anyone   cardboard   milkshake

popcorn   dustbin   grandfather

paintbrush   somebody   handbag

Silent letters

A **silent letter** is a letter in a word that we do not hear when we say the word.

lam**b**   **k**nife   **g**nome

whale   yo**l**k   **w**reck

Here are some more examples of words with **silent letters**.

answer	guitar	knock
wheat	bomb	knee
scissors	rhyme	write

Top spelling tips

1. If you are stuck spelling a word, use a dictionary to help you. The alphabet chart on page 6 can help you locate the word.

2. The letter **q** is always followed by the letter **u**.

queen   quilt   quill

3. There are no words that end in the letter **v**.

4. This well-known spelling rule usually works:

i before e except after c

Here are two examples:

f**ie**ld (**i before e**)

rec**ei**pt (**except after c**)

But remember there are some w**ei**rd exceptions!